A taste for *Life*

food for body and soul

lesley ramsay

recipes: rachel billington   photography: christine semple

A Taste For Life: food for body and soul
© 10Publishing 2015

Published by 10Publishing, a division of 10ofthose.com
9D Centurion Court, Farington, Leyland, PR25 3UQ, England

Email: info@10ofthose.com
Website: www.10ofthose.com

ISBN 9781906173050

Cover design Lankshear Design Pty Ltd.

contents

introduction

I love good food. I love eating (too much, at times). I love shopping for enticing, fresh ingredients. I love creating an interesting array of luscious dishes for friends and family, to be consumed over many hours of conversation with a good wine. I love to linger last of all over a cup of espresso and fine chocolate, not wanting the night to end.

I also love life. What a wonderful gift we hold in our hands – to live and breathe, to swim and bushwalk, to read and think, to debate and make music, to serve and contribute to others, to love and be loved. And I love the God who is the Giver of all these good things.

In this book I have tried to bring these 'loves' together. The language of hunger, taste, satisfaction and contentment finds echoes in life as well as food. I want to introduce you to the Great Chef – God. He conjures up a meal that nourishes us and relieves our hunger. He entices us with ... *a taste for life*. Life that lasts.

As you read, take time out to head for the kitchen and cook the tempting recipes we have provided. There is a recipe for everything from entrees to biscotti with coffee.

I hope you enjoy reading, thinking, cooking, eating. I hope you will discover *a taste for life*.

thank you

It has been great fun co-operating on this book with some good friends.

Rachel's recipes had my mouth watering from the time I first read them – and then tasted them. Thank you, Rachel, for your commitment to good food.

Christine Semple's attention to detail as she styled and photographed the food was amazing. Thank you, Christine, for 'pushing' us for the sake of excellence.

Many, many thanks to Angela Cole for her phenomenal way with words as she made my feeble attempts readable.

Thank you to Natalie Ray for being so open and honest in sharing her story with us.

Judy Chapman was very generous with her lovely house that we invaded for the 'photo shoot' – thank you.

To Jim, my best friend, confidante and husband – thank you for everything you are for me and do for me. Thank you, especially, for your suggestions that have made this a better book than it would have otherwise been.

Above all, thank you to God, who loved me enough to satisfy my desperate hunger, and to make me his own.

hummus dip

- **1 can chick peas (drained) or 1/2 cup fresh chick peas that have been soaked**
- **1/2 teaspoon ground cumin**
- **2 tablespoons lime juice and grated rind of 1 lime**
- **1 teaspoon crushed garlic**
- **2 tablespoons tahini paste (sesame paste)**
- **up to 1/2 cup olive oil**

method

Blend all ingredients together in a food processor until smooth. Add oil last, a little at a time. Depending on the taste and consistency you like, add as much as necessary up to the 1/2 cup.

Chapter 1 | relishing food

Food: | foōd |

noun
any nutritious substance that people or animals eat or drink, or that plants absorb, in order to maintain life and growth[1]

We know we need to eat to stay alive. Even newborn babies perceive enough to cry when they are hungry; instinct tells them that it's dangerous not to eat.

When reduced to its essentials, food is a conglomerate of proteins, carbohydrates, minerals, vitamins and undoubtedly other things I am unaware of. If necessary, we could possibly consume these vital elements in a once-a-day capsule in order to survive.

But that would be a travesty of beauty and pleasure. For food – a wonderful gift of the Creator God – is meant to be savoured and enjoyed, not merely ingested to 'maintain life'.

Under God's extraordinary hand of design, taste is arguably the most evocative of the senses. It is charged with memory, emotion, desire and sometimes aversion.

Relish for a moment the thought of freshly baked bread, of quality vanilla bean ice-cream crowned with ruby red strawberries, of comforting roasted winter vegetables dressed in garlic and honey, of tender beef in a creamy massaman curry, of golden mango cheeks …

Would God create such a spectacular assortment of eye-catching beauty, mouth-watering tastes and delightful aromas if we were not meant to enjoy food?

Certainly, food does have the utilitarian purpose of keeping us alive; yet it is so much more than that!

Food looms large in our shared and personal experiences: from the food that is first identified in our cultural history – the piece of fruit that Eve chose – right through to Jamie Oliver's mission to rescue good food from foolish humanity.

Sociologists and anthropologists study the culinary practices of people groups across the globe. Journalists report and debate statistics about nutrition and health. On a food critic's whim, restaurants will open and close with astounding frequency.

On a more personal level, we celebrate a milestone like a wedding anniversary with an intimate dinner by candlelight, or we throw a sensational party for a 21st or 40th birthday.

When we meet to chat with a friend, we are most likely to do so in a cafe over a latte and a friand.

Food is often a means of telling someone we love them. My husband's all-time favourite comfort food is lemon meringue pie, and when I go to the extraordinary lengths that I do to make it, he knows that I really do love him!

Then there are the times when we are miserable or depressed. What is it that we inevitably reach for? Chocolate. Someone once said that nine out of ten people like chocolate, and that the tenth person always lies!

According to Jamie Oliver, food is all about relationships:

> *At the end of the day, (my book) is for everyone who is interested in cooking tasty, gutsy, simple, commonsense food and having a right good laugh at the same time. That's what food's all about. It's not just about eating. To me it's about passing the potatoes around the table, ripping up some bread, licking my fingers, getting tipsy and enjoying the company of good friends or family. Pass us the mustard, Dad.*[2]

But there's a dilemma with food ...

ENDNOTES

1 "Food" Def. New Oxford American Dictionary, 2nd ed.
2 Jamie Oliver, The Return of the Naked Chef, Penguin Books, 2002, p11.

caramelised onion tarts

makes 24
preparation time: 20
cooking time: pastry 20
cooking time: filling 30-45

- 1 quantity shortcrust pastry or ready-made shortcrust pastry sheets cut into small rounds
- 3 thinly sliced onions
- 2 tablespoons butter, melted
- 2 tablespoons balsamic vinegar
- 2 tablespoons brown sugar
- 150g danish feta cheese
- 2 eggs
- 150ml thin pouring cream
- salt and pepper to season

method

Melt butter in pan and add onions, cooking until clear. Add vinegar and sugar. Reduce heat and simmer for about 30–40 minutes until thick and dark in colour. It's hot and will burn you, so no tasting this off the wooden spoon!

Line mini-muffin pans with pastry and blind bake (i.e. place small pieces of greaseproof paper into each piece of pastry and add 1 teaspoon of raw rice or some pastry weights. Bake in oven at 180°C for 10 minutes, then remove paper and rice and cook for 5 more minutes.)

Put caramelised onion into cooked tart cases and add a small piece of crumbled feta. Mix eggs and cream together and top each tart with a little of the mixture. Return to oven for a further 15 minutes to cook.

Actually, there are several dilemmas that converge around food: our love of junk food rather than wholesome food; our over-indulgence leading to obesity, or our rejection of food leading to anorexia; the fact that so many throughout the world simply go hungry …

But it's another dispiriting aspect to food that is my focus here. Let me explain.

What is your ultimate food pleasure? The flavour you have grown to delight in above all others? I wonder if you can remember the first time you encountered it?

My ultimate food pleasure is chocolate – any kind, but especially dark chocolate with nuts. I don't remember when I first discovered this sweet sensation, but I do have a wonderful recollection of my grandson, Nathan, when he was about nine months old. His mother had some chocolate on her finger and he licked it off. His eyes became wide and alert, as if spellbound. The look on his face seemed to ask: *'What was that and where do I get more?'*

What is your favourite taste luxury?

Here is mine. I've finished my work for the night and am about to sit down to read or watch a little TV before I head off to bed. I make a cappuccino in my coffee machine, add a splash of creamy coffee liqueur, and carefully unwrap a special chocolate – perhaps a Ferrero Rocher or a Guylian. The routine then becomes: take a sip of coffee, then a bite of chocolate, a sip, a bite – always ending with the last sliver of chocolate. I lie back and let the rich, creamy taste linger in my mouth.

Do you know the worst part of that little extravagance, though? Before I go to bed I have to clean my teeth! The seductive taste and sensation are gone! As I climb into bed, I think to myself, *'The pleasure was so short-lived I may as well not have had it!'*

It's like that with a good deal of our effort in the kitchen, isn't it? I remember spending hours one day preparing and cooking a special, exotic meal for some friends. We had had an amazing meal at their place, and I wanted to make a good impression in return. I don't remember the first two courses, but I do the last.

It was back in the days of 'bombe Alaska' – an ice-cream and meringue dessert famous for the spectacular special effects created when brandy was poured over it and set alight! I carried this glorious creation into the dining room with flames leaping in the air. It really was a magnificent pièce de résistance – the perfect finale for the night. At the end of the evening, we settled into a wonderful vibe of conversation over coffee and chocolate, completely satisfied and contented.

BUT the next morning, we were all hungry again and needing to tuck into tea and toast, or whatever we usually ate for breakfast. The magnificent meal of the night before became a faint memory in the rush of a new day. I doubt that any of my guests that night remember the meal now. The experience was short-lived. The hunger returned.

Some friends of mine recently told me of being taken out for dinner to a very classy 'high-end' restaurant. Their business acquaintance hosts paid the equivalent of the GDP of a small country for the meal and alcohol! My friends were embarrassed.

BUT, the next morning, they were all hungry again. Thousands of dollars had exchanged hands, yet they were right back where they started.

You know as well as I do why I linger over the Guylian and cappuccino, and why I spent hours in the kitchen over the bombe Alaska, and why a small fortune is transacted every day in restaurants all over the country.

Because good food tastes so good! If only it would last.

CONTINUED PAGE 16

page 13

roasted vegetable stack

serves 4
(as an entree)
preparation time: 10
cooking time: 30

- 1 eggplant, sliced
- 2 roma tomatoes, sliced
- 2 small zucchini, sliced thinly length ways
- a few pieces of butternut pumpkin, sliced thinly
- 1 red capsicum, halved and seeded
- 150g feta cheese, or baby bocconcini
- a little olive oil
- sea salt and black pepper

DRESSING

- 2 teaspoons chopped basil
- lemon juice to taste
- 2 teaspoons brown sugar
- 2 tablespoons balsamic vinegar
- 4 tablespoons olive oil

method

Preheat oven to 200°C. On a baking sheet lined with baking paper, roast all vegetables with a little olive oil and seasoning in the hot oven for 20-30 minutes. If the skin of the capsicum burns and blisters, remove it.

To make dressing, combine all ingredients and mix well. Stir again before drizzling over stack.

To assemble the stack, place 4 serving plates in front of you. Layer the roasted vegetables on each one, starting with the eggplant, then tomatoes, zucchini, pumpkin and capsicum. Then add a piece of feta or bocconcini. Repeat the process until all the vegetables have been used, finishing with a layer of feta. To give the stack stability place the larger pieces of vegetables at the bottom, moving up the stack to finish with the smallest pieces. Drizzle a small amount of dressing over each stack.

This can be served warm or at room temperature.

Even the enjoyable company of good friends and family that motivates Jamie Oliver to cook good food won't last forever. We 'fall out' with our friends over trivial hurts. Significant relationships break down. Eventually friends and family die. We die.

It is not surprising, then, that God – food's Creator and Provider – should choose the imagery and language of food to describe a hunger of much greater significance than that related to our physical nutrition.

A hunger for life. A hunger for relationship. A hunger for acceptance.

More nourishing still, He offers complete satisfaction.

A taste for life. Life that lasts.

Chapter 3 | hungry?

What is the hungriest you've ever been?

I remember one day returning from a bushwalk – a recreational activity that our family often enjoyed together. (It was cheap for a family of six, lasted all day and thoroughly exhausted the kids!) On this occasion, we'd miscalculated the distance (it was **much** longer than we thought) and not taken nearly enough food to get us through. We dragged ourselves that last couple of kilometres with our stomachs rumbling and our tongues hanging out. We were ravenous!

Maybe you've felt famished during the first week of a crash diet when your stomach craved something more than celery and cottage cheese.

But do you know what it feels like to be desperately hungry? Missing not just an occasional meal, but eight or ten meals in succession?

Oliver and his pals in the orphanage did:

Food, glorious food!
Hot sausage and mustard!
While we're in the mood –
Cold jelly and custard!
Pease pudding and saveloys!
What next is the question?
Rich gentlemen have it, boys –
In-di-gestion!

Food, glorious food!
Don't care what it looks like –
Burned! Underdone! Crude!
Don't care what the cook's like.
Just thinking of growing fat –
Our senses go reeling
One moment of knowing that
Full-up feeling!

Food, glorious food!
What wouldn't we give for
That extra bit more –
That's all that we live for
Why should we be fated to

CONTINUED PAGE 20 ☞

asian-influenced tuna

serves 6-8
preparation time: 10

- **450g tuna**
(firm deep-red tuna is best)
- **1 ripe avocado,**
peeled and diced
- **juice of 4-5 limes**
- **1 fresh chilli, seeds**
removed and finely chopped
- **3 tablespoons**
sesame seed oil
- **4 tablespoons coconut milk**
- **1 bunch fresh coriander,**
finely chopped, reserving
some for garnish
- **3 tablespoons**
sesame seeds
- **a little finger of ginger,**
peeled and finely chopped
- **soy sauce**
- **French stick or**
some toasted Lebanese
bread to serve

method

Dice tuna into 2cm cubes and place in a bowl. Add remaining ingredients and stir, adding soy sauce to taste. Garnish with coriander or chilli.

The tuna will not be raw – the acid in the lime juice will begin to cook the fish.

Do nothing but brood
On food,
Magical food, wonderful food,
Marvellous food, fabulous food! [1]

For Oliver, food was a matter of life and death. He didn't care whether it was burned or underdone – he just wanted that 'full-up feeling'!

That was life for 19th century street orphans, and sadly it is still life for the 820 million people who go to sleep each night hungry. Every five seconds a child dies because she or he is hungry.

These are confronting and appalling statistics. But there is another hunger that besets many more than the poverty-stricken. It actually affects all of us, because we are all creatures.

I am going to make a fairly bold statement. **Every human was made to live in relationship with the Creator of the universe.** The famous atheistic writer, Richard Dawkins, would no doubt be quite dismayed right now if he were reading over your shoulder.

But bear with me for a moment.

If you are very honest with yourself, there have probably been times in your life when you have wondered: *Is this all that life has to offer? Sure, I may have enough food on the table to feed my family well. Yes, I may live in an air-conditioned house with all the mod cons and I may be able to take that trip to Bali. But is that all there is? Am I just born, only to grow, live, work, retire and then die?*

What you are sensing is 'spiritual hunger'.

We find ourselves hungry because we do not experience life as it was meant to be – that is, lived out in friendship with the living God who designed us and knows exactly what we need to thrive.

I read once that we can identify three stages of hunger. First there is a sensation of emptiness – a gut feeling that makes us long for food. Then there is a gnawing restlessness, like an animal that has not been fed. It paces up and down, gets desperate, claws at the cage. Finally, weakness sets in. A person without food can't work. He or she simply lies down helplessly.

The spiritually hungry often find themselves going through the same stages.

To begin with, there is a vague, unsatisfied longing for meaning in life. We sense a lack of destiny or purpose. The trivia of 21st century life seems mind-numbing. There is a deep sense of feeling lost and empty. We sense something is missing but are unable to identify exactly what it is that's not there. Our spiritual 'stomachs' grumble, but we always think there is another good meal around the corner. Sometimes there is, but the satisfaction doesn't last long.

The second stage of spiritual hunger is a real restlessness. It can feel like deep sobbing from the very centre of our soul. We pace up and down like a caged animal. We try this and we try that – anything that we can get our hands on. That is why people delve into Zen Buddhism, or astrology, or new sexual experiences. We rush into some cause to save the world, or splurge on shopping we can't afford, or fly off sightseeing. But nothing satisfies.

The third stage is when apathy takes hold. We become bored, lethargic. There is no zest for life. We lose the capacity to enjoy anything at all. We think about ending it all. We wish we could die.

In the movie *Notting Hill,* Julia Roberts plays the role of Anna Scott – a famous Hollywood actress who is thought to have a life and a lifestyle that most people would kill for.

But there's one scene where she says to Hugh Grant's character, William:

> *"I'm 29 years of age and I've been on a diet since I was 19, which means that I've been hungry for 10 years. I've had a series of not very nice boys. And every time my heart gets broken the media make a circus out of it. I've had to have two painful operations to look like this, and one day I won't be wanted by anyone."* [2]

The internal void Anna expressed so honestly is summed up in this quote from Al Gore:

> *The accumulation of material goods is at an all-time high, but so is the number of people who feel an emptiness in their lives.*[3]

Are you hungry?

ENDNOTES

1 Selected lyrics from *Food, Glorious Food* from the musical Oliver! by Lionel Bart.

2 *Notting Hill*, Dir. Roger Mitchell, Writ. Richard Curtis, Working Title Films, 1999.

3 Al Gore, *Earth in the Balance,* Houghton Mifflin, Boston, 1992, pp. 221-222.

Chapter 4 | running on empty

Surely the big question is: *Why are we hungry?* We know there is something missing, but have we ever explored the reasons?

It all has to do with **how** we got here and **who** was responsible for it.

We humans are physical beings and we live in a material, temporal world. We therefore need the basics of survival: food, rest, clothing and shelter.

We also have a sub-stratum of 'needs': recreation, comfort, achievement at work, romantic relationships, aesthetics, sensual pleasure and so on. Not vital, but nice to have.

Yet this is not the sum total of all that we are. We are also spiritual beings— created in God's image and needing a personal relationship with God above all else. This relationship with God is the integration point around which all these other things find their rightful place.

Ultimately, if this relationship is not in place, all of the perishable 'food' in the world is not enough to keep the hunger at bay.

This whole process started at the beginning of history. It's recorded for us in the very first book of the Bible, called Genesis. There, you can read how God created people – bearing his image – to rule the world under him, and placed them in an idyllic, perfect place called the Garden of Eden. God promised to love them, take care of them and provide them with everything they needed. They in turn would trust him completely, love and honour him, and be obedient to him.

In this perfect setting, life was satisfying – hunger was utterly foreign to them. They loved and depended on God for everything; he loved them and always acted in their best interests.

They were happy and contented

CONTINUED PAGE 26

moroccan lamb with couscous and yoghurt

serves 4
preparation time: 15
cooking time: 10

- **4 Small lamb fillets or back straps**

MARINADE

- **2 tablespoons moroccan spice mix**
- **1 cup red wine**
- **200g couscous**
- **1 litre strong chicken stock**
- **30g butter**
- **80g currants**
- **roasted pumpkin or blanched beans**

DRESSING

- **300ml natural yoghurt**
- **1 teaspoon garam masala (an Indian spice mix)**
- **2 teaspoons honey**
- **fresh mint, finely chopped**

method

Combine Moroccan spice and wine together in a flat dish and mix well. Marinate fillets for at least 1 hour; the longer they are marinated, the better the taste.

Cook marinated lamb under grill or on a BBQ for 10 minutes, turning once during cooking. (Lamb should be served pink). Serve lamb on bed of couscous and top with yoghurt dressing.

To prepare couscous, add butter to raw couscous in a bowl. Gently add the hot chicken stock to couscous and butter, a little at a time, continually stirring until couscous is fluffy and cooked. Use a fork to prevent it sticking together. Add the currants and stir well. Season with salt and ground black pepper. Roasted pumpkin or fresh blanched beans may be added to couscous for an extra touch. Serve hot.

To make dressing, combine all ingredients and serve drizzled over the top of the lamb, or as an accompaniment.

because they trusted God. They needed nothing else.

But as time went on, they began to want more – more power, more control, more say in what they did and how they did it.

That little voice of temptation said to them: *You can take control of your own lives. You can make your own decisions about what is right and wrong. You do not need to merely accept what God says. Do not be content with trusting what God says. Find out for yourselves! Do your own thing.*

Therein lay the origin of spiritual hunger.

You see, these people didn't need anything else to live happily.

The great deception – the great lie that they swallowed – was that they did need something more; and spiritual hunger set in. The tragedy is, they acted on their discontent. They thought that the only way they could be satisfied was to go outside of God; and that's what they did.

They stopped trusting him and rebelled against him. The heartbreaking consequence of that rebellion was that they were cut off from him – no longer friends.

They were cut off from their source of satisfaction – God himself – and destined to be always searching for that elusive 'something' that would satisfy them.

Isn't that exactly the position that you and I find ourselves in today?

God seems distant from us – elusive; or worse, we don't even want to know him, and we ignore him. We find ourselves cut off from our source of satisfaction – God.

It's as if there is this huge hole inside us, and we try desperately to fill it. But the truth is it's a God-shaped hole, and no matter what we keep putting in it, nothing can really fill it like God can.

We find ourselves caught on this treadmill – chasing – catching something – then chasing again.

Have you ever seen a little caged mouse on one of those circular treadmills in a pet shop window? Their little feet are running 'hell for leather', but they stay in the one place. They expend endless energy, but it's pathetically pointless.

Our situation is like that. We are never satisfied. We find ourselves at times with that gnawing hunger at the core of our being. Yet the great deception – the great soul-destroying lie that we have swallowed – is this: *Chase everything to try and satisfy your hunger, but don't chase God. He's irrelevant.*

So we turn our backs on him and push him out of our lives. This is a terrible insult to God. It offends him and it hurts him.

Meanwhile, we find ourselves in a barren, parched wasteland, longing for 'a good meal' to fill the emptiness inside.

Chapter 5 | filled to overflowing

Is true satisfaction just a myth? A rumour you might hear on the streets? Or could it be that somewhere our spiritual hunger can be filled?

The answer to both questions is 'no'. True satisfaction is no myth, nor is it a rumour. But neither can you go somewhere to find it. It can only be found in **someone**.

Let me relate for you a story – and more importantly a true story.

The action takes place sometime between 30 and 33AD, on the shores of the Lake of Galilee across from a city called Capernaum in Palestine.

This story involves a crowd – a very large crowd of some thousands of people who have come to an isolated spot to catch a glimpse of a man they believe to be quite out of the ordinary.

The man is Jesus.

Now before I can go any further with my story, I need to take you back in time a few months earlier. At this point, Jesus had been living for 28 years in relative obscurity in a town called Nazareth. Then one day, he burst onto the consciousness of his neighbours. He stood in the town synagogue and read this excerpt from the Jewish scriptures:

> *The Spirit of the Lord is on me,*
> *because he has anointed me*
> *to preach good news to the poor.*
> *He has sent me to proclaim freedom*
> *for the prisoners*
> *and recovery of sight for the blind,*
> *to release the oppressed …*

Then he looked at them and said:

> *"Today this scripture is fulfilled in your hearing."* [1]

The good folk of Nazareth were stunned; gobsmacked. Wasn't this just the son of the carpenter, Joseph, who lived on the other side of town? And wasn't his mother Mary, that non-descript woman they saw at the market?

Yet by claiming that this description applied to him, Jesus was saying that he was the special person chosen by God to rule God's world. He was to be the one the Jews had been waiting for: the Messiah. It was a declaration of Jesus' mission – the purpose for which he has been sent by God.

But just what was the good news that the poor were going to hear? Which prisoners were going to be freed? How could the blind receive their sight?

What we need to understand is that Jesus was not talking primarily about physical poverty or blindness or imprisonment. Rather, his presence in the world would confront the awful realities of spiritual poverty, spiritual blindness, spiritual captivity, and – in the language we've been using in this book – spiritual hunger.

It's clear, isn't it, that all is not right with the world? Five minutes in front of the television news convinces us of that.

Terrorism, rape and corruption are the international markers of our problem. But we hardly have to look that far afield. Each of us knows that life is not all that we had hoped it would be for us or those we love: cancer, drug addiction, marriage breakdown, despair.

Spiritual poverty. Spiritual blindness. Spiritual captivity. Spiritual hunger.

The people of Jesus' day were unsure how he was going to deal with problems like these, but were they in for a roller-coaster ride! What they would witness over the following months would turn out to be a pointer to who Jesus really was. He would give back sight to the blind, enable life-long cripples to run again, restore hearing and speech to the deaf and the mute, transform leprous flesh to fresh, healthy tissue, and even reverse death!

But back to our story!

The crowd has followed Jesus because they are fascinated by these healing miracles. Maybe he will cure me … or my little boy?

CONTINUED PAGE 32

page 29

crisp-skinned chicken with pancetta and herb stuffing

serves 4
preparation time: 20
cooking time: 20

- **4 chicken marylands, skin on (breast fillet with leg still attached)**
- **olive oil**
- **1 onion, diced**
- **1 teaspoon crushed garlic**
- **2 teaspoons fresh chopped flat-leaf parsley**
- **1 teaspoon chopped or dried sage**
- **150g chopped pancetta or prosciutto**
- **150g fresh breadcrumbs**

SAUCE

- **200g tub mascarpone**
- **2 tablespoons pesto**

method

Preheat oven to 200°C.

Heat a little olive oil in a frying pan. Add the chopped onion, garlic and herbs and cook for 2 minutes. Add the pancetta or prosciutto and cook until crisp, then add breadcrumbs. Set aside to cool a little.

Gently slip a finger under the skin of each chicken piece; merely loosen it without totally removing it. Place equal amounts of the stuffing under the skin of each chicken piece and chill for a few minutes.

Heat a little olive oil in large frying pan and place each piece of chicken skin side down into the pan (only 2 at a time to prevent reducing the heat in the pan too much). Sear for a few minutes on each side. Then transfer onto a baking tray and finish cooking in oven for 15 minutes or until completely cooked though.

You can serve sauce cold (as in illustration) by simply mixing mascarpone and pesto together. To serve warm, combine the two over a low heat in the same frying pan, stirring all the time until reduced slightly. Drizzle over the chicken. Yum!

However that constant companion, hunger, has crept up on them, and Jesus' friends wonder where on earth can they get enough food to feed so many thousands.

This is not a problem for Jesus – it is actually a great opportunity. He takes five small bread rolls and two small fish – in effect a young boy's lunch – and turns it into enough food for more than 5,000 people. Not only do they have a full and complete meal, but there are twelve baskets of food left over!

It's easy to understand the crowd's response. They want this man as their leader. Not because they like what he says, or what he stands for, or because they want to start obeying the God he talks about, but because he filled their bellies! Food, glorious food – and it didn't cost a thing! Besides, if he can do it once, maybe he can do it again and again!

Things gather pace now. Jesus and his friends escape from the crowd determined to make him king, and cross to the other side of the lake.

But this is one very persistent crowd. The memory of all that food that Jesus conjured out of nothing is creating intoxicating images in their minds. The prospect of always having their desires met is a powerful catalyst for action. They move quickly and soon find him.

Read this quote from the Bible to see what happens next:

When they found him on the other side of the lake, they asked him, "Rabbi, when did you get here?"

Jesus answered, "I tell you the truth, you are looking for me, not because you saw miraculous signs but because you ate the loaves and had your fill. Do not work for food that spoils, but for food that endures to eternal life, which the Son of Man will give you. On him God the Father has placed his seal of approval."

Then they asked him, "What must we do to do the works God requires?"

Jesus answered, "The work of God is this: to believe in the one he has sent."

...Then Jesus declared, "I am the bread of life. He who comes to me will never go hungry, and he who believes in me will never be thirsty." [2]

Jesus knows why they have come looking for him – they want him to take on that role of forever satisfying their physical needs: *Whenever we want food, just provide it Jesus. We'll never be dissatisfied again, and we'll have you as our king forever.*

Any normal person would welcome this sort of attention and adulation and gladly give them what they want. There's no doubt he could. But not Jesus. He knows that satisfying them at this level is not good for them, because although it would stem their physical hunger, their spiritual hunger would remain untouched.

Instead, he presents them with some startling advice that will deal with their real problem.

Firstly, *"Do not work for food that spoils."*

Here is a great indication that as glorious as food is, it just does not measure up! Jesus is not only talking about food literally, but anything physical that we really desire and work hard for. We work incredibly hard and invest a great deal of energy into acquiring 'stuff', only to see it one day spoil or rot away or be destroyed or disappear.

I remember hearing of a couple who were moving up the affluence ladder: buying a house, and then after a couple of years selling it to buy a bigger and better one, until finally they got the house of their dreams. No matter that the kids were no longer spending much time at home anymore – their five-bedroom, three-bathroom mansion with a home theatre was what they'd always wanted!

The mortgage contract stipulated they had to have home insurance, but their fittings and new furniture meant they had nothing left over for contents insurance. You can probably guess where I am going. They arrived home one night to find the house and everything in it in smouldering ruins. Their dream had been reduced to ashes: food that spoils.

CONTINUED PAGE 36

page 33

flourless chocolate torte with berry coulis

serves 8
preparation time: 20
cooking time: 40-50

- 175g good quality dark chocolate, chopped
- 150g soft unsalted butter
- 100g caster sugar
- 6 large eggs, separated
- 150g ground almonds
- a drop of vanilla essence
- 300g frozen or fresh raspberries
- 3 tablespoons icing sugar

method

Preheat oven to 180°C. Grease and line a 23cm round spring-form tin.

Chop the chocolate and melt on low heat in microwave or in a bowl over some boiling water. Leave to cool.

Beat the butter until soft, then add 50g of the sugar and cream together. Add egg yolks one at a time while still beating, then slowly add the cooled melted chocolate, ground almonds and vanilla. Beat together.

Whip egg whites until stiff and add remaining 50g caster sugar to the whites while still whisking. Add a small amount of cake mixture to the whites and fold in. Repeat this bit by bit, until all the cake mixture has been added.

Pour into tin and bake for 45-50 minutes. Don't expect a cake tester to come out clean as this is a rich, dense cake. Allow cake to cool in its tin for 30 minutes, then remove and serve.

For the berry coulis, puree the berries in a food processor or with a hand blender until smooth, and add sugar to taste. Sieve the mix if you prefer a really smooth texture, otherwise it's delicious as is. Serve over the cake with cream or ice-cream.

Then there was the woman who was always dissatisfied with her job – the work, the atmosphere, the money. Nothing really met her expectations. Finally, she got the job – no, not just the job, the position of a lifetime! Surely now she would be happy till her retirement. A month after she started, the company was merged with another and she was made redundant in the reorganisation: food that spoils.

What was Jesus' alternative? This is his second piece of advice: *"Work for food that endures to eternal life"*.

You see, the problem with food that spoils is that it is only temporary. The satisfaction may last a few hours, a few weeks, even months or years, but it's not going to last forever.

That's why we experience hunger (physical and spiritual); what we rely on for satisfaction is only temporary. This is the exact opposite of that which endures to eternal life.

When Sydney celebrated the dawn of the new millennium on New Year's Eve 1999, the Sydney Harbour Bridge was lit up with the word 'Eternity'. That remarkable image was flashed right round the globe, and people were asking, *'What does it mean?'*

The word was written all over Sydney's streets early last century by a man called Arthur Stace. Arthur was a man who was desperately hungry and had tried to find satisfaction in all sorts of ways, mostly from the neck of a bottle. In the process, he had become a hopeless, homeless alcoholic. Until one night, he wandered into a church and heard a talk about Jesus and realised there was a life beyond this one. He discovered that there was an existence that never ended that was inhabited by God, and he wanted to be part of it. Even though he was virtually illiterate and couldn't write more than a few scratches, Arthur Stace wrote the word 'Eternity' in beautiful copperplate writing thousands of times all over Sydney. It was his testimony to the fact that he had found the remedy to his spiritual hunger.

Eternity. Eternal life. Life that goes on

forever. Life lived for God and with God. A relationship with God that began that night. A relationship that he was made for. A relationship that never ended.

Jesus says that's what you chase after.

Then comes Jesus' jaw-dropping claim in the last sentence:

Jesus declared, "I am the bread of life. He who comes to me will never go hungry, and he who believes in me will never be thirsty."

Here is the ultimate in gratification – a **person** who says they are the bread of life.

In other words, you will be satisfied if you 'feed' on this bread. Deep down inside satisfied. Remember that hole deep inside of us? The God-shaped hole? Only God can fill it. Your heart is restless until it rests in him. Having a relationship with Jesus satisfies now, and lasts into eternity.

You need not go on with that gnawing hunger in your soul. Hear and respond to the invitation of the God who made you for himself:

"Come, all you who are thirsty,
   come to the waters;
and you who have no money,
   come, buy and eat!
Come, buy wine and milk
   without money and without cost.

Why spend money on what is not bread,
   and your labour on what does not satisfy?
Listen, listen to me, and eat what is good,
and your soul will delight in the richest of fare.

Give ear and come to me;
   hear me, that your soul may live ..." [3]

Come to Jesus, the bread of life.

ENDNOTES
1   The Bible, The Gospel of Luke, Chapter 4, verses 18-19, 21.
2   The Bible, The Gospel of John, Chapter 6, verses 25-29, 35.
3   The Bible, The Book of Isaiah, Chapter 55, verses 1-3.

Chapter 6 | believing

Did you notice the question the crowd in Chapter 5 asked? *"What must we do to do the works God requires?"*

That's the question I had, too.

It's a very important question, because if it is possible to find satisfaction, and to sustain it so that I'll never be hungry again, then I want to know how to get this *'food that endures'*.

Jesus' answer is absolutely breathtaking. *"The work of God is this: to believe in the one he has sent"*.

'Remember the scene in the synagogue at Nazareth? The one God has sent is Jesus. So his cut-to-the-chase answer is: believe in Jesus.

Hang on. Is it that simple? Is that all I have to do? Lots of people say they believe in Jesus but still seem to be desperately hungry. I'd agree. But make sure you know what it means to 'believe in Jesus'.

There was once a great stunt highwire artist called Charles Blondin. In 1859, he stretched a tight rope across Niagara Falls and walked across it. He was the toast of America: *"The greatest tightrope walker that has ever lived!"* screamed the headlines. He proceeded to ride a bike across the wire **and** to do it blindfolded.

A newspaper reporter came to interview him after he announced he would push a wheelbarrow across the Falls.

"Do you believe I can do this great feat?" Blondin asked the reporter.

"I really do believe. You are the greatest tightrope walker of all time!"

"Well then," said Blondin, *"you get in the wheelbarrow and come with me!"*

There was silence. The reporter made a hasty retreat as the implications of his brash statement dawned on him.

There's a world of difference between believing in something or someone in theory, and being willing to commit your life into his or her hands.

Believing in Jesus means two things.

Firstly it means recognising who he is. Jesus and his disciples testify that he was the one sent by God to our planet to be born and live as the God-man among flawed humans. As God's much-loved Son, he had enjoyed a privileged position in the splendour of heaven, living and ruling with his Father. On earth, he didn't merely live, but lived perfectly, always honouring and obeying his Father.

At the end of his short life, he allowed himself to be arrested by scheming men and then submitted to the indignity and shame of death by crucifixion. And why? Because out of love he chose to pay the penalty for our rebellion – that deep offence we've caused God by refusing to seek him and chasing after food that doesn't satisfy instead. Every human that has ever lived deserves to personally suffer the consequences of offending God. But Jesus absorbed the punishment himself so that people could be forgiven and know God as their Father; so that they wouldn't be hungry any more. God placed his seal of approval on all that Jesus had done by raising him from death to be the Lord of the universe.

Acknowledging all this is believing in Jesus in theory. Lots of people do this and it doesn't make a shred of difference.

Ultimately, believing requires something more. Believing in Jesus is saying to him: *"I'm a bit afraid here; this is a big step for me. But I'm going to trust you with my life. I'm going to rely on you to forgive my rebellion. I want to be restored to a close relationship with God. I'm not going to go searching for things that can't satisfy me any longer. I'm going to give up my self-reliance and now rely on you for everything."*

That's believing in Jesus in practice. Some do this, and it makes **all** the difference.

I recounted the story of Blondin to someone once, and he retorted that it was unfair to judge the reporter for not jumping into the wheelbarrow. After all, he may have trusted Blondin's competency, but how could he trust the things over which Blondin had no control? The quality of the tightrope, for example. Or the weather? Or the soundness of the wheelbarrow?

That's a fair comment. Blondin couldn't guarantee those variables. But there is nothing that is outside of Jesus' control. There are no variables with Jesus. Because he, along with his Father, is the Creator and Sustainer of life; nothing will take him by surprise. Once we believe, events may seem shaky from our viewpoint, but Jesus will have us firmly safe, soundly satisfied and eternally secure.

Can you see it now? Believing is actually trusting and relying on Jesus, and it is absolutely essential to being satisfied.

However, if I were to leave it there, I would be doing you a disservice. It would be like telling an unhealthy person who has eaten junk food all their life that there is fantastic food out there that tastes wonderful, is easy to get, and will make you amazingly healthy in a flash. The truth is,

they cannot have all the benefits of good food without some changes to their life. They need to stop the regular visits to Maccas, or give up bingeing on pizza and ice-cream in front of the TV.

Trusting in Jesus may be simple, but it's not easy. For trusting Jesus also means following Jesus. It means you will need to change – humbling yourself to ask for forgiveness for your rebellion, trusting and relying on him, and then putting him first in your life from now on. It's saying 'no' to the junk food addiction in your life choices, and saying 'yes' to the great food he will give you.

Do you trust what he says? What have you got to lose? Do you want to feed on the true and life-giving bread so that you will never go hungry again?

Here are some words you could say to God (a prayer, if you like) …

God, I am so **sorry** that I have lived as if I was in control of my life and have looked for satisfaction outside of you. I know I have offended you and deserve your punishment. I want this life of hunger and rebellion to end today.

God, I want to say **thank you** for loving me and sending Jesus to die on the cross in my place. Thank you that he paid the price for my rebellion and that I can now be forgiven and come into a father-child relationship with you. Thank you that you raised him from the dead and that he lives as Lord and King of this world. Thank you that through Jesus you have satisfied the great hunger of my life.

God, **please** help me to live with Jesus as my King from now on, bringing honour and glory to him.

hazelnut berry meringue stack

serves 8
preparation time: 10
cooking time: 60

- **6 egg whites**
- **350g caster sugar**
- **75g ground hazelnut meal**
- **400ml thickened cream, whipped**
- **450g frozen or fresh mixed berries**
- **50g grated chocolate or 1 cadbury flake**

method

Whisk egg whites to soft peak consistency, then gradually add sugar to the whites while still whisking until all the sugar is dissolved. The mix should be thick and glossy. Add the hazelnut meal, folding in carefully.

Line two baking trays with foil. Place half the mixture on each tray and spread in a circle about 30cm wide. Place the mixture in a cold oven (heated to 140°C) for 1 hour, then switch oven off and leave in overnight or for at least 3 hours.

Remove from foil and place one half on a flat, round platter. Spread with a layer of half the whipped cream and half the berries. Place the second meringue circle on top and press down gently. Repeat cream and berries, and finish with the chocolate or Flake.

Fill just before serving to ensure the meringue stays crisp. Slice to serve.

For a small dinner party, you could make individual 'stacks'.

Chapter 7 | taste and see

One of my favourite Mediterranean restaurant dishes is the tapas plate. Tapas are designed to be succulent starters to arouse the appetite, but I've found them a wonderful opportunity to sample a great range of flavours and textures, thus expanding my culinary experience.

When my children were young, they would look suspiciously at some new food I was trying to introduce and insist on 'having a taste' rather than simply take my word for it that it was going to be delicious.

We often need some prior exposure to something before we commit wholeheartedly, so it is not surprising that God invites us to come and 'taste' what he has to offer.

One of the great poets of the Bible, a man named David, wrote:

Taste and see that the LORD is good; blessed is the man who takes refuge in him.[1]

Unfortunately, the common misconception about God in our world is that he is a cross between a 'wowser' and a heavenly policeman. He doesn't want us to have fun and has a long list of arbitrary rules we have to follow. If we transgress, then he will come down on us 'like a ton of bricks'. We will lose our freedom, our capacity to think, our enjoyment of sex ...

In London recently, the British Humanist Association commissioned an ad for display on the sides of 800 buses and on 1,000 posters in the underground railway system. They carried the slogan: *"There's probably no God. Now stop worrying and enjoy your life."*

If this is what people think God is like, then they have clearly not taken the time or the effort to investigate his true character. They have not 'tasted'. Like small children, they have rejected great food because they were too frightened to 'taste and see'.

In fact, when we begin to explore what God is like, and who Jesus is and what he has done for us, we are presented with a 'gourmet banquet'. We find ourselves contemplating a good and generous God who longs to give us a rich and full life.

Dip into God's tapas plate with me; let's sample what he has to offer for those with the courage to 'taste and see'.

Firstly, defying all the stereotypes, he wants to give us freedom, not take it away from us. He promises freedom from the tyranny that rebellion towards him has over us; freedom from guilt over the way we've treated him and the people we love; freedom from the anger and pain we feel when we think life has served us a raw deal; freedom from the confusion and fear that beset people when they think this life is random. He gives us the freedom to grow and serve and love him, and to love those around us in a way that enriches them, not stifles them. Jesus said, *"... If the Son sets you free, you will be free indeed."*[2]

Taste and see that the Lord is good.

As for fun, what a great gift God has given us! The ability to smile and laugh and enjoy good humour comes from the Creator himself. But God's gift of joy is so much deeper than fun.

Joy is being able to say – at even the blackest of times – that my God holds onto me, and nothing that the world throws at me will ever separate me from him. It is the knowledge that God is sovereign (that is, he is powerful and in control) and nothing will happen unless he says so! I may be in pain, I may be grieving, I may be disappointed, I may be feeling threatened, but my joy will be complete because I am satisfied and secure in him.

Taste and see that the Lord is good.

And does it surprise you to hear that God invented sex? It was all his idea – and certainly enjoyment of sex is part of the deal! There's a book in the Bible called *Song of Solomon* which celebrates the sexual relationship between a husband and his wife. It makes for interesting reading!

It goes without saying that because sex is his idea and his creation, he knows best how it will work for his people. When sex is abused and used selfishly to gratify an individual's desires, we move outside of God's good intentions for sex.[3]

Taste and see that the Lord is good.

As for rule-keeping, it's impossible to deny there are many laws in the Bible. Jesus was once asked which was the greatest rule of all.

He replied:

'Love the Lord your God with all your heart and with all your soul and with all your mind.' This is the first and greatest commandment. And the second is like it: 'Love your neighbour as yourself.'

All the Law and the Prophets hang on these two commandments.[4]

In other words, if only we would truly love and honour God with all that we have, and then love and regard everyone else just as we do ourselves, then there would be no need for any other rule or law.

But it is patently obvious that we don't do that. We can't do it because of the problem we considered earlier – our rejection of the trustworthy and true God as the only one who can completely satisfy us, and who has the right to demand our unrivalled allegiance.

So God's law in the Bible serves two purposes.

One, God graciously gives us boundaries and restrictions to protect us. Without them we would annihilate each other! Imagine if someone like Adolph Hitler had lived with no moral law to be accountable to. I shudder to think!

Two, the law serves to highlight how far we have strayed from God and how seriously we have offended him. It keeps pointing out to us how guilty we are. This is a great thing, because ultimately we realise we are in a desperate situation and that our only hope is in Jesus.

Taste and see that the Lord is good.

There is one other thing about God that people often mention leaves them with a 'bad taste in the mouth'. It is the fact that one day people will face the judgement of God. How could judgement and its accompanying punishment possibly be good?

Judgement implies accountability: to be held to account for our attitudes and actions. Again, imagine a world without accountability. Humans would do unspeakably terrible things. One of my son's friends was murdered on his way home from school several years ago – stabbed for a wallet containing $5. The police believe they know who his killer is, but they do not have enough evidence to charge him. So will he just get away with murder? No, because one day he will face God as his judge who has all the evidence! That boy's mother knows that one day her son's killer will face the consequences of his terrible deed.

Accountability gives meaning to all that we do. It prevents our world being a place of haphazard meaninglessness. However it means we are held to account, too: for treating God as irrelevant and chasing after the trivialities of life to satisfy us; for not loving God with all our heart and soul and mind; and for not trusting Jesus to forgive us. Personally facing God – with all our rebelliousness fully exposed – will not be a pleasant thing! But as I have explained in Chapter 6, Jesus absorbed the punishment of those who rely on him in his death on the cross. The bitterness of God's judgment becomes an enticing morsel when combined with Jesus' sacrificial death.

People often want God to be like Santa Claus or a kind, old grandfatherly figure who doles out goodies but never holds us to account. Yet that would be a caricature

– and certainly a wimpy, tasteless no-God!

Taste and see that the Lord is good.

The best I have saved until last: the loving kindness of God. In one of the most magnificent depictions of God in the Bible, he is described as the one *"who is rich in mercy"*.[5] Because of his great love for us, God extends his mercy to us and forgives us even though we deserve the opposite!

Don't you love that word 'rich'? For me it conjures up succulent taste sensations laden with excess – perhaps the thick ganache coating a chocolate mud cake, or a heavy sauce with lashings of double cream swirled throughout. Definitely the sort of food that *Weight Watchers* would recommend you consume in moderation. As for God, he lavishes his mercy on us every day and we can only thank him for his lack of restraint!

His mercy is most supremely seen in the death of his son. Neither you nor I are worthy of forgiveness. We do not deserve to have our hunger satisfied by the Lord

Jesus. We are not deserving of a deep-seated joy. Yet he died so that forgiven humans might live!

Taste and see that the Lord is good.

Have you sampled enough from my tapas plate of God's goodness to want to know him better? Has it whet your appetite for discovering more about Jesus? The good news is this remarkable meal can continue forever! Don't be content to stop now. Try something more substantial. Delve deeper.

Go to the best place possible to get to know God better – the Bible, where he speaks for himself. Let the last word go to that ancient poet, David, who so savoured the life-giving words he found there:

How sweet are your words to my taste, sweeter than honey to my mouth! [6]

ENDNOTES

1   *The Bible,* The Book of Psalms, Chapter 34, verse 8.
2   *The Bible,* The Gospel of John, Chapter 8, verse 36.
3   If you want to read more on this subject, you could try *Pure Sex* by Tony Payne and Philip Jensen. Available from http://www.matthiasmedia.com.au
4   *The Bible,* The Gospel of Matthew, Chapter 22, verses 37-40.
5   *The Bible,* The Book of Ephesians, Chapter 2, verse 4.
6   *The Bible,* The Book of Psalms, Chapter 119, verse 103.

coffee hazelnut biscotti

makes about 30

preparation time: 20

total cooking time: 60
(35 plus 25)

- 1 cup (220g) caster sugar
- 2 eggs
- 1 1/3 cups (200g) plain flour
- 1/3 cup (50g) self-raising flour
- 1 tablespoon espresso-style instant coffee powder
- 2 teaspoons hot water
- 1/3 cup (35g) hazelnut meal
- 1 cup (150g) hazelnuts
- (Variation: use 1/2 cup chopped dark chocolate and 1/2 of hazelnuts)

method

Roast hazelnuts in medium to hot oven until lightly browned, then rub the nuts together in a tea towel to remove the skins.

Whisk sugar and eggs together in a medium bowl. Stir in flours, combined coffee and water, hazelnut meal and hazelnuts. Divide dough into 2 portions. Using floured hands, roll each portion into a 20cm log; place on lightly greased oven trays. Bake in a moderate oven (180°C) for about 35 minutes or until firm; cool on tray.

Cut logs diagonally into 1cm thick slices using a serrated knife. Place slices, cut side up, on oven trays.

Bake in moderately slow oven (160°C) for about 25 minutes or until crisp and dry, turning once during cooking; cool on trays.

Ideal for 'dunking' in coffee!

Chapter 8 | natalie's story

It was somewhere around the time that I moved from childhood to puberty that I became angry at God.

My mum had died when I was 2. Initially, my views of God and spiritual things were bound up with what I had been told about my mum: she was now with God as an angel in heaven, floating with ribbons streaming from her hair …

But as I looked at my world with new eyes, disillusionment overwhelmed me. I was angry that God – whoever or wherever he was – had taken my mum from me. I hadn't deserved that; he was cruel and vindictive.

And so on the cusp of adulthood, I rejected any notion of God and began to experiment with alternative spiritualities. I found an entry into Goth culture, and from there, neo-paganism and white witchcraft. The world seemed empty to me – even bleak – and I was convinced there must be more to life than mere existence.

The great attraction of witchcraft was the power it promised to give me as an individual to summon elemental powers and forces to do my bidding. Through witchcraft, I thought I had found myself – that I had power and that I was in control. It seemed as if a whole new world of possibilities had opened up for me.

However, the further I was drawn into witchcraft, the more I realised those promises were empty, and that I was still restless, unfulfilled, and struggling with grief and anger. In the end, I never settled completely into witchcraft, and my spiritualism morphed into a fascination with contacting the dead. I was lonely and desperately missed my mum, and I wanted to believe that contacting her was the way to fill the hole I knew was there. I investigated near-death and out-of-body experiences. But they were also barren, and

I found myself sinking slowly into despair.

Looking back now, I can see that witchcraft and spiritualism never really held any satisfactory answers for me. There was so much focus on the individual and how to channel power, money and happiness for oneself; they were instant gratification philosophies. In my experience, they did not grapple with the underlying issues behind people's searching, and hence could not satisfy my hunger.

But a chance encounter with an old friend turned my world upside down. During the course of our conversation she told me she was a Christian, which caused me to immediately launch into a hostile attack on her. I had been a debater at school and had gained a reputation for being quick on my feet and verbally aggressive. I remember thinking she was stupid for her faith, and accusing her of grovelling in the presence of her so-called God in order to earn her way into heaven. My friend was very patient and kind to me, and at one point she said something that stopped me in my tracks. She said, "I can't earn my way to heaven. Jesus died as a gift – there is no way I deserve it. Your understanding of Christianity is just not true."

Jesus died as a gift. I didn't know what this really meant, but the idea that Christianity was not about earning your way to heaven was completely new to me, and it was deeply unsettling. It started me thinking.

She ended up inviting me to come to a Christmas musical at church and I accepted, really because I was curious. Now, going to church was a serious threat to my identity as a Goth. I made sure I turned up in my blackest Goth outfit, even down to the white talc and black make-up on my face. As I watched these Christians – many of them friends from school whom I had mercilessly persecuted – I could tell there was something different about them. For one thing, they were totally accepting of me, not once alluding to my terrible

CONTINUED PAGE 56

classic cosmopolitan cocktail

Serves 4-6

- **400ml cranberry juice**
- **400ml dry ginger ale**
- **150ml white rum for alcoholic version; OR soda water**
- **Crushed ice to serve**

method

Mix all ingredients together and serve immediately over crushed ice in martini glasses or long tumblers.

The cranberry juice may be substituted with orange or guava juice, but technically it will no longer be a 'classic cosmo'.

classic

cosmo

treatment of them. It was a generosity I certainly didn't deserve.

After the musical (which I thought was pretty lame), a man named Neil gave a short talk about the importance of the birth of Jesus – God who was born as a baby and would one day die as a gift. There it was again: gift. Following this, they sang 'Joy to the world, the Lord is come' and the penny dropped. I suddenly understood that the reason these Christians were so excited about Christmas was because it was a celebration of God being born into the world as a man – a man who would later die on a cross so that I could be made right with God. This was the truest thing I had ever heard, and I suddenly realised that here was hope – real hope. Nothing I had ever heard, read, or experienced before this came anywhere close. At last, I had discovered how to ease the hunger I had experienced for so many years. On that night, I gave up trying to control my life and committed that responsibility to God.

That was 11 years ago, and in the time since, I have come to an understanding of the world and my place in it that makes complete sense. I have real peace, real hope, and a real assurance of spending eternity with God, who is my loving Father – the one who sent his Son to die for me. My spiritual hunger for something to make sense of the world has been satisfied by a person – Jesus Christ.

If you would like to make a comment about the book or ask a question feel free to email ENC at **info@newchurches.org.au**